SHAKESPEARE'S PROPHETIC MIND

SHAKESPEARE'S PROPHETIC MIND

By

A. C. HARWOOD

RUDOLF STEINER PRESS

1st Edition, Rudolf Steiner Press, 1964
2nd Impression, Rudolf Steiner Press, 1977

Made and printed in Great Britain by
The Camelot Press Ltd, Southampton

APPROXIMATE CHRONOLOGY OF THE PLAYS

(Not including plays only partly by Shakespeare)

1593 Love's Labour's Lost. Comedy of Errors. Taming of the Shrew. Two Gentlemen of Verona.

1594 Romeo and Juliet.

1595 Midsummer Night's Dream. Richard the Second.

1596 King John. The Merchant of Venice.

1597 First Part of Henry the Fourth.

1598 Second Part of Henry the Fourth. Much Ado about Nothing.

1599 Henry the Fifth. As You Like It. Julius Caesar.

1600 Troilus and Cressida. Merry Wives of Windsor.

1601 and 1602. Twelfth Night. Hamlet.

1604 All's Well that Ends Well. Measure for Measure. Othello.

1606 Macbeth. Lear.

1607 Antony and Cleopatra. Coriolanus. Timon of Athens.

1608 Pericles, Prince of Tyre.

1610 Cymbeline.

1611 Winter's Tale. The Tempest.

Shakespeare was 28 in 1592: 35 in 1599: 42 in 1606.

Hear the voice of the Bard!
Who present, past, and future, sees;
Whose ears have heard
The Holy Word
That walk'd among the ancient trees,

Calling the lapsed soul,
And weeping in the evening dew;
That might control
The starry pole,
And fallen, fallen light renew.

WILLIAM BLAKE

SHAKESPEARE'S PROPHETIC MIND

THE thesis of this book is a very simple one. It is a belief that a poet has a prophetic character and that the greater the poet the more he prophesies. I do not mean that he prophesies actual events, though prophet and poet were combined in the ancient bard or vates, and the *Sortes Vergilianæ* show us that the Middle Ages clung to this old tradition. I mean he is prophetic in the sphere of consciousness. He lives intensely in those powers of feeling and apprehension which he has inherited from the past, he carries them into new forms which influence and even create the experience of his day, and (if he is great enough) he leaves a seed dropping from the ripeness of his powers which, like the fabled wheat in the pyramids, may only germinate after long centuries. This last is certainly true of Vergil in whom there is a power of painting with tones, of suggesting by the tensions and sympathies between words, which is hardly to be found again before Shakespeare himself.

If it is objected that the present and the past have nothing to do with prophecy, I have my answer ready and, like the staid elder brother in Comus, I call antiquity from the old schools of Greece. For Homer, knowing what a prophet must be, tells us that Teiresias knew alike the past, the present and the future. Perhaps all vision into the future depends on knowledge of the past and experience of the present. Was it accident or genius that linked three figures with Shakespeare in the doggerel Latin on his tomb in Stratford-on-Avon?

Ingenio Pyladen, Socratem mente, arte Maronem.

7

In wisdom a Nestor (Pylades)—Nestor who always lived in his memories of the past. In mind a Socrates—Socrates who was the midwife of ideas, in every present moment delivering a new child of the mind. In art a Vergil (Maro)—Vergil the prophetic poet of whom Shakespeare's age still believed that he had foretold the coming of the Christ child. Here is past, present and future presented by three Worthies, to grace Shakespeare's tomb, as they might have graced the end of one of his plays.

Terra tegit, populus maeret, Olympus habet

Earth, men and the heavens, the realms of body, soul and spirit. Are we being told to think of Shakespeare as a master of this trinity as well?

There will always be a hard core of Shakespeare criticism which is concerned with literary, historical and factual problems. But this criticism is almost irrelevant to the appreciation of the plays, and can throw no light on the fact that different centuries have found different interests and values in the plays, and that the modern age is once more looking at Shakespeare with fresh eyes.

For what did Shakespeare's own age especially value him? They plainly enjoyed his humour and his bawdiness, much of which is lost on modern playgoers who do not understand his vocabulary or his topical allusions. But essentially, I believe, they liked the picture of life lived at full stretch and its expression in splendid language—the great word spoken on the great occasion, as it has never been spoken in the theatre since. They were not offended by the wildness which the eighteenth century sought to tame. Indeed it is difficult to imagine what appreciation that century could have had of Shakespeare when we know it preferred to see *Hamlet* or *Lear* acted with a happy ending. Perhaps even so it found in the plays an escape into a larger world than reason and its own limited theatre permitted it. Voltaire could not accompany his contemporaries so far. In his *Letters on England* he wrote* that while Shakespeare was natural and sublime 'he had not one spark of good taste, or knew one rule of the drama'. Indeed he considered that the influence of Shakespeare had been the ruin of the English stage.

Nineteenth century critics were largely interested in studying the development of character, as befitted the age of the novel. It is to be feared, however, that they sometimes found such development where it does not exist. Schoolboys are still tested on their critical standards. It is in our own century that a new note has begun to sound. Some critics have begun to speak of the plays as 'meditations' or 'mysteries' in which a deep understanding of life stands behind the immediate picture of the drama. I think such critics are right, and that to think of particular plays in this way—I shall deal with some of them— adds greatly to our appreciation of them as dramas, just as I believe Professor Wind has added greatly to our aesthetic appreciation of such a picture as Botticelli's *Primavera* by revealing the thought which lies behind its form.† But I believe we can also appreciate each individual play the better, if we can see it in its place in the development of the plays as a whole.

In this development I see something greater than the progress of an author's mind. A great change in human consciousness had begun, affecting not only what but how men thought and felt. It is a process which is far from ended, and one in

* Letter XVIII.
† Edgar Wind. *Pagan Myths in the Renaissance*, Faber & Faber.

which we are still called to take part today. It is this universal process, destined to affect all mankind, which Shakespeare, through the universal quality of his imagination, experienced more deeply than any man of his time, and to which he gave expression in the sequence of his plays.

In Shakespeare's time a very old established world with its roots in Greece, and before Greece, was being challenged by the new humanism and the new science, and the old and the new rubbed shoulders together without much consciousness of difficulty. Bacon, the father of a new philosophy of science, could still cure his warts by sympathetic magic, rubbing them with fat on a piece of animal skin, and then hanging the fat to be melted in the sun. For years after Shakespeare's death the most incompatible notions shared common beds, even the Royal Bed of the Father of Scientific Societies. All this only goes to show that a slow (but not *very* slow) change of consciousness was in progress. Shakespeare inevitably took part in this change: but as the poet who soon came to hold the primacy among poets, who never goes out of fashion, who reveals something new to every succeeding age, he did more than take part in it: he led it, and to a large extent created it. I do not mean that he knew he was doing it, or that people who saw or read his plays knew they were learning new modes of consciousness from them. We learn most when we do not know we are learning, like a child breathing in the world through his pores. We teach most when we do not know we are teaching, but when we are totally devoted to some work in hand. It was this kind of learning and teaching which passed between Shakespeare and his audience. Men who saw his plays saw a total picture of man, and it was a picture in continual development.

We can, of course, say that the changes were due to the circumstances of Shakespeare's life, that, after a high spirited youth (not without its troubles) he went through a period of disillusionment, and that he grew serene and contemplative in his old age. Personal life may colour or condition genius, but it cannot explain it. The real question is: What does genius do with the personal life? The answers are varied. Sometimes genius uses it, sometimes it annihilates it. But with Shakespeare, happily enough, we know so little of his personal life that the question need not even be asked. All we have to do is to read, or see, his work, and try to understand it with our modern consciousness. We deceive ourselves if we think it is easy to do so. For Shakespeare stood at one of the great frontiers of consciousness, the almost impenetrable gulf between the mediaeval and the modern age. In crossing that frontier man entered a world where he finally abandoned the deepest belief of antiquity, which the Middle Ages inherited from the Greeks, the Greeks from Egypt and Chaldaea, and Egypt and Chaldaea from the unrecorded infancy of man. It is the belief in the innate sympathy between things, in the same creative principles and forces working in the universe, in the earth and in man, the belief that the part of the whole is not only a part (as in the machine) but is in some degree a miniature of the whole, and above all that man himself is a small universe, a microcosm of the macrocosm. We are the first civilisation which does not live in the daily experience of that belief. Our trees and minerals no longer embody planetary virtues, the zodiac no longer forms and sustains our bodies, nor do the elements live in our dispositions. We have divorced the understanding of man from the understanding of the universe, because we have divorced man himself from the universe. Know thyself, said the Delphic oracle, and thou wilt understand the world. We endeavour, and we are the first to do so, to understand the world without first understanding ourselves.

CORRESPONDENCES

Shakespeare's age still took for granted all this lore of microcosm and macrocosm which we have forgotten; though modern scholars (without believing in it) have discovered that, without some knowledge of it, many of the plays lose much of their bite and flavour.* It is to be found *passim* in all his plays, and Shakespeare assumes a knowledge of it in his audience. Even the groundlings were expected to know that the frame of the human body from top to toe was created by the forces of the Zodiac from the Ram to the Fishes. When Sir Toby Belch insinuates that Andrew Aguecheek's excellency in a galliard is because he was born under Taurus, Aguecheek asserts that Taurus is 'sides and hearts'. 'No,' says Sir Toby, 'it's legs and thighs—let me see you caper.' The modern audience may echo the actors' stage laugh, but probably neither appreciate the point—that both Sir Toby and Aguecheek are wrong. Taurus is 'necks and throats', and indeed Sir Toby gives the truth away by using the word 'caper'. It is the Goat (Capricorn) which forms the leg, and to caper has its name thence.

Such allusions may be found throughout the plays, but it is undoubtedly in the earlier plays that the belief in the 'correspondences' between the great and little worlds plays a full and determining part, or, to be definite as to time, in the plays generally agreed to have appeared between 1592 and 1599, that is, in terms of Shakespeare's life between the ages of 28 and 35.† These include *Love's Labour's Lost* (which some think the first complete play), *Romeo and Juliet*, *The Merchant of Venice*, *A Midsummer Night's Dream*, and the English Histories, of which the sequence from *Richard II* to *Henry V* is alone authentic Shakespeare. It is among these plays that

* Cf. Professor Tilyard: *The Elizabethan World Picture.*
† I follow in general the chronology of Sir E. K. Chambers.

we find the supreme examples of the ancient belief in a universal order playing into the life of man and the earth from the heavenly order of planets and fixed stars.

Romeo and Juliet

The best known of these beliefs (and one which survives in some quarters even to the present day) is the ruling of man's destiny by the stars. This is the theme of *Romeo and Juliet* (1594). To Romeo the Gods allow a flash of insight into his star-given destiny. As far as his normal consciousness is concerned he is going to the Capulet ball to see his Rosaline. But before the party of young gallants set out there is a significant scene* where he speaks of a warning he has had in a dream that he should not go. Mercutio puts it aside with his high-spirited description of Queen Mab, and the party is about to set on when Romeo stops them. A chill comes over the scene, as when a dark cloud, unnoticed, suddenly eclipses the summer sun, and Romeo speaks:

> 'my mind misgives
> Some consequence yet hanging in the stars
> Shall bitterly begin his fearful date
> With this night's revels, and expire the term
> Of a despised life clos'd in my breast,
> By some vile forfeit of untimely death:
> But He, that hath the steerage of my course,
> Direct my sail. On, lusty gentlemen.

For a moment Romeo's dream consciousness has broken through into his waking mind. He has brought with him a knowledge of his destiny, but he is not allowed to escape it.

Twice at least Romeo returns to the theme of his star destiny.

* Act I, Scene 4.

When he hears of Juliet's supposed death, and intends to shorten his fated span of life, it is with the words: 'I defy you, stars!'

Finally, in the tomb:

> 'O here
> Will I set up my everlasting rest,
> And shake the yoke of inauspicious stars
> From this world-wearied flesh'.

Here we are still fully in the world of 'correspondences'. Man and the stars are one. It is only when we reach the end of this first seven year epoch of Shakespeare's writing that another note creeps in. Thus Cassius in *Julius Caesar* (1599):

> 'The fault, dear Brutus, is not in our stars,
> But in ourselves, that we are underlings'.

And thus Helena in *All's Well that Ends Well* (1604):

> 'Our remedies oft in ourselves do lie
> Which we ascribe to heaven: the fated sky
> Gives us free scope; only doth backward pull
> Our slow designs when we ourselves are dull'.

In *Lear* (1606) it is true that Gloucester blames eclipses for the evils of Society. But the new and insistent voice is with Edmund, who echoes Hotspur's contempt for signs and portents.

> 'This is the excellent foppery of the world, that when we are sick in fortune—often the surfeit of our own behaviour—we make guilty of our disasters the sun, the moon and the stars: as if we were villians by necessity, fools by heavenly compulsion . . . an admirable evasion by whoremaster man, to lay his goatish disposition to the charge of a star!'

Lear himself, who might so well have claimed to be the

victim of Fortune and the Stars, insists on the contrary that he
has worn out whole

> 'packs and sects of great ones
> That ebb and flow by the moon'.

This was all fairly new doctrine—or heresy—in Shakespeare's
time and must have had for his hearers something of the
flavour of Ibsen and Shaw daring to tilt at social conventions in
their age. But Shakespeare does not end with the 'freedom
from the stars' which has given modern man his final sense of
personal responsibility. In *The Tempest* (1611), the last of
Shakespeare's complete plays, Prospero points to an even
higher freedom, the freedom to use the celestial influence
consciously. (The freedom of the man who sails with the wind
is greater than the freedom of the man who rows himself.)
That man must match himself to the hour is Prospero's creed.

> 'I find my zenith doth depend upon
> A most auspicious star, whose influence
> If now I court not, but omit, my fortunes
> Will ever after droop.'

Hermione in *The Winter's Tale* (of the same date) had already
said the same in corollary.

> 'There's some ill planet reigns:
> I must be patient till the heavens look
> With an aspect more favourable.'

We shall find the same outlook in that little known and
scarcely ever acted play, *Pericles*, which ushers in the last
period of Shakespeare's writings.

This is neither the acceptance of Romeo, nor the modern
contempt of the Bastard Edmund. Already we have a glimpse
of something that may yet await man if once again he comes to
look upon the universe with his imaginative or spiritual eye
and not his physical alone. It is not to command the compulsive

15

power of the stars as the old astrologers wished to do, but to attune human affairs to the rhythms of the universe.

To return to Romeo, by some dramatic principle of palingenesis Shakespeare chose for this, his first tragedy, a theme of blood guilt down the generations such as might have made a trilogy on the Greek stage. Shakespeare's play, however, differs from a Greek drama not only in being a single play, but in the character of the solution. It was the tragedy of the ancient world that even the Gods demanded that blood should be avenged by blood. Orestes is commanded by Apollo to murder his mother in order to avenge his father, but he is none the less guilty of a crime, for which he is tormented by the Furies. How was the cycle to come to an end? The Greek solution was to bring Orestes before the Court of the Areopagus, presided over by Athene herself, who alone could settle the necessary rites of purification, and, in so doing, turn the Furies into the Gracious Ones, the Eumenides. This solution would hardly satisfy us today, when guilt is not acquired through enforced action, nor do external ceremonies purge it away. To appreciate it, we have to break our way into a world where the principle of the 'eye for the eye' was still the natural principle. We must remember that the human institution of Law was then a new and radiant birth, worthy of the reverence accorded to a God. We must remind ourselves that Athene, alone of the Gods, did not belong to the stream of the generations but sprang fully armed from the head of Zeus. She therefore represented a power which man received direct from the spiritual world, not through heredity, and this power alone could unbind what the blood had bound. But the more we place ourselves in sympathy into this pre-Christian age the more we feel how impossible was such a solution for the age of Shakespeare. The alchemy of the Being who was Love had slowly changed the world. The new solution has to be brought about through the principle of love, even if in the immediate picture of the play it is an instinctive love. But there is a hint of an even deeper meaning to those who follow a stream of thought which issues from Plato and beyond, that the human soul descends at birth from a spiritual existence and even takes some part in choosing the path of life which appears on earth as its destiny.* To such, the lovers, Romeo and Juliet, may appear as two human souls who have chosen their fate, in order that through sacrifice they may break the chain of the blood-feud. Thus the play ends with the hand of Montague clasped in the hand of Capulet.

Montague
> For I will raise her statue in pure gold,
> That whiles Verona by that name is known,
> There shall no figure at such rate be set
> As that of true and faithful Juliet.

Capulet
> As rich shall Romeo by his lady lie
> Poor sacrifices of our enmity.

Shakespeare leaves us with the picture of reconciliation and atonement won through love and sacrifice.

We should contrast this final with the opening scene of the play, where first the servants and then the scions of the two houses start an affray immediately on meeting. The picture, as often in Shakespeare's plays, speaks as eloquently as the words.

The Merchant of Venice

If *Romeo and Juliet* is essentially a play of human destiny written in the stars, a play concerned with the laws of time, *The Merchant of Venice* is concerned with the abiding 'correspondences' in space between things terrestrial and celestial. The play has been described by Professor C. S. Lewis as a

* *The Myth of Er* at the end of the *Republic*.

meditation on metals, but metals, of course, in the high mediaeval sense where the Sun is gold, the Moon silver, Mercury quicksilver, Saturn lead,

> 'And Mars is iron and Jupiter is tin,
> And Venus copper, by my faderkin.'

In this play we are concerned also with 'Primacies', the belief that in each kingdom of Nature, and each organic family, there is subordination or degree in which one member holds the primacy. Among the planets, the Sun: in human society, the King: among animals, the lion: among land-birds, the eagle: among sea-birds, the osprey: among flowers, the rose: among metals, gold: of the life-organs, the heart: of the senses, the eye: among the four elements, fire. The speech of Ulysses in *Troilus and Cressida** describes forcibly the evils that arise in the elements, in human society, in the human soul, when degree breaks down.

> 'Take but degree away, untune that string,
> And, hark, what discord follows.'

For Shakespeare's audience this splendid speech, with its appeal to the still active experience of the correspondence of the Sun and King, of fever in the body and in the state, must have been overwhelming. For us these things have become mere metaphors.

The Merchant of Venice, however, does more than allude, in however powerful a manner, to Correspondences and Primacies. It is built up on them. But we do not observe it if we stay at the level of the obvious contrast between the noble Antonio and the scheming Jew. Sometimes Shakespeare seems consciously to invite us to 'look on this picture and on that'. We may enjoy the picture of wife-taming in the *Shrew*; or we may reflect that

---

* Act I, Scene 3.

18

this play is chosen for the special delectation of the drunken sot, Christopher Sly. Similarly in the *Merchant*, remembering that a Jewish doctor had recently been supposed to have poisoned the Queen, we may cry with the groundlings, Down with the Jew. But if we look more carefully, we may see that there is a contrast in the play far deeper than that between scheming Jew and noble Christian. It is the contrast between Belmont, the Fair Mountain, and Venice, the mercantile city on the plain. In Venice, even though Antonio pays lip service to the mediaeval Christian view on interest, the 'breed of barren metal', he behaves in a most unchristian manner to Shylock, calling him cur and spitting on his Jewish gaberdine. Unrepentantly he declares: 'Yea, and am like to do the same again'. In Venice, Bassanio is a mere fortune hunter, seeking an easy way to liquidate his debts. In Venice, Jessica is a mean little thief, stealing, not only her father's ducats and jewels, but even the ring which Leah had given him before their marriage: and this ring, as a crowning indignity, she changes for a monkey! In Venice, Lorenzo, praises her as a 'Gentile and no Jew', when she gilds herself with still more stolen ducats. They are not a high-minded lot in the City on the Plain.

But on the Fair Mountain the spirit of Portia prevails.

> 'her sunny locks
> Hang on her temples like a golden fleece;
> Which makes her seat of Belmont, Colchos' strand,
> And many Jasons come in quest of her.'

The quest of Portia is a spiritual quest, as was the quest of the Argonauts. Bassanio, who came frankly for a fortune, has to forget gold and silver and choose what threatens rather than what pleases. For Portia needs nothing to enhance her heart qualities of love and generosity. With what generosity she despatches Bassanio to the relief of his friend on the very day of her wedding! With what circumspection she prepares to bring the qualities of the Fair Mountain down to the City on the Plain! And there, while Shylock is demanding the flesh which lies next the heart (the heart itself has perhaps too much of the Sun), Portia urges in contrast the spiritual or heavenly quality of the heart, the quality of mercy, which drops like the gentle rain from heaven.

> 'It is enthroned in the hearts of kings,
> It is an attribute to God himself.'

Here we have a double primacy—heart and king—which leads us to the greatest of all primacies, God himself. It is only when the appeal to the heart has failed that the law is turned against the seeker of the law. But the Duke has heard the call to Mercy (is he not a king?) and in despite of the vindictive Gratiano, Shylock's life at least is spared.

The return to Portia's realm of Belmont is one of the most beautiful things in Shakespeare. The magic of the Fair Mountain has wrought its alchemy on the rapacious Lorenzo and Jessica. The reiterated use of the sound '*s*' evokes the stillness of the summer night. Lorenzo speaks:

> 'How sweet the moonlight sleeps upon this bank!
> Here will we sit and let the sounds of music
> Creep in our ears: soft stillness and the night
> Becomes the touches of sweet harmony.
> Sit, Jessica. Look how the floor of heaven
> Is thick inlaid with patines of bright gold:
> There's not the smallest orb which thou behold'st
> But in his motion like an angel sings,
> Still quiring to the young-eyed cherubins.'

It is only on the mountain, and only in the stillness of the heart that we can see the heavenly gold and hear the music of the spheres, to which our 'Venice' as well has closed our eyes and shut our ears. Be still, said the psalmist, and know that I am God.

The last scene of the play, with its spirited jest of the rings, brings us back to gold—not the gold of Venice, 'the pale and common drudge 'twixt man and man', but the gold which binds human heart to human heart, the loss of which we should fear more than anything in the world.

> 'Well, while I live I'll fear no other thing
> So much as keeping safe Nerissa's ring.'

THE ENGLISH HISTORIES

As long as mankind kept even the poor remnant of that original experience of union with the universe which lived in the correspondences, he could not know the isolation out of which alone the fulness of freedom can be born. That early man 'lived together' with Nature and with his tribe in a kind of common consciousness is increasingly acknowledged by anthropologists today. It has been called 'participation mystique' by Lévy-Bruhl, and from a more philosophical point of view 'original participation' by Owen Barfield.* What was really taking place behind all the inner and outer changes which separate our age from the mediaeval was the final abandonment of participation with the result that nature became something external to man, something with which he could experiment and about which he could form his own independent theories. Realism, which still bound man's thinking to a universal world of thought, gave place to nominalism. Man the Participator became man the Spectator.

The Shakespearian stage reflects the fact that drama is now concerned essentially with the individual. The Greek stage had

* Cf. *Saving the Appearances* (Faber and Faber).

three levels each representing a plane of consciousness. Below in the orchestra was the Chorus with its communal consciousness still informed by the constant presence of the divine, mystically sensitive to the impending fate, living in ancient memories. Above was the sphere of the Gods ever ready to intervene in human affairs, representative of the divine machinery of the earlier Epic. Between the two, on the stage proper, were the human actors, meeting each other as individuals, struggling with their inter-related destinies out of a purely human consciousness, not yet as wise either as the Gods or as the Chorus with its dim forebodings and intuitions. Now there was to be a new stage with only one level of consciousness where man was to be represented in the full exercise of his independent powers. This was the stage of Shakespeare's central plays, in which he transcends the 'participation' themes of his earlier plays to create the supreme figure of the Spectator in *Hamlet* (1601).

But before we reach this middle epoch of the Plays which Hamlet inaugurates, and in which lie the great studies of individuals such as Lear, Macbeth and Othello, something else is to be taken into account. The mind of the individual is always related to the mind of the people in which he is born, and the mind of the people depends to a greater or lesser extent on the land where that people lives. Who of those who have experienced it can doubt that the special quality of the light in Greece, which penetrates and irradiates the very stones, was a necessary condition of the luminous Greek mind? The Greek mind, however, still felt itself able to reach the Ideas of the Divine Mind. Thinking, for this very reason, was in itself a guarantee of truth, because it could reach that level of consciousness represented on the Greek stage by the level of the Gods. The modern Spectator Consciousness is independent and isolated. The Spectator is in fact an island from which he looks out through his senses on an alien world. England, which mediated the Spectator Consciousness into human experience, is itself an island, and one of the first steps in the development of that consciousness is that the English begin to feel it as an island. The Norman-descended Baronage had for long felt the Channel as something which united them—in peace or war, as friend or hostage—with their peers abroad. Now there arises the feeling that the Channel is something that gloriously protects and isolates. We hear it in *King John* (1596) from the point of view of the foreigner, Austria.

> 'that pale, that white-faced shore,
> Whose foot spurns back the ocean's roaring tides,
> And coops from other lands her islanders'.

But, the year before, it has come in *Richard II* (1595) from the dying John of Gaunt as a prophetic utterance—he speaks as 'a prophet new inspired'—on his death bed in a splendid piece of rhetoric.

> 'This precious stone set in the silver sea,
> Which serves it in the office of a wall,
> Or as a moat defensive to a house,
> Against the envy of less happier lands.'

Ben Jonson called England 'the world the world without' and it was easy to quote Vergil (prophetic Vergil)

> *Et penitus toto divisos orbe Britannos.*

Indeed something of the neo-Platonic theory of the union of opposites entered into the idea that Britain was central to Europe because it was eccentric, and that Britons were free because they were confined. In the late seventeenth century, Lord Halifax attributed England's world-power to its isolation. 'Happy confinement' he wrote, 'that has made us free.'

Perhaps we may see in the course of English history a

progressive development. First the consciousness of England itself as an island: then the happy belief that 'the Englishman's house is his castle': and last the sad cry of final isolation from the lips of one who best expressed the nostalgia of his century for the irrecoverable participation of man with nature, the lost union of man with man.

> Yes, in the sea of life enisled,
> With echoing straits between us thrown,
> Dotting the shoreless watery wild,
> We mortal millions live *alone*. . . .

But this isolation is part of human destiny

> A God, a God their severance ruled!
> And bade betwixt their shores to be
> The unplumb'd, salt, estranging sea.*

It was a prophetic cry that Shakespeare put into the mouth of John of Gaunt. For England in Gaunt's day still lived in the dream of territorial union with France. But if we look at the Histories from *Richard II* to *Henry V* we see with what accuracy of vision Shakespeare traces in the miniature field of English history a microcosm of the great process, enacted in the whole story of man, which separated him from the Gods, and brought him the terrible responsibility of freedom. Richard II still lives in the mediaeval world of correspondences. His subjects—even his rebel subjects—still speak of him as bearing the primacy of rule. 'Be he the fire' says Bolingbroke, 'I'll be the yielding water.' Then later:

Bolingbroke
> See, see, King Richard doth himself appear
> As doth the blushing discontented sun . . .
> When he perceives the envious clouds are bent
> To dim his glory . . .

* Matthew Arnold: *Isolation. To Marguerite.*

24

York

> Yet looks he like a king. Behold, his eye,
> As bright as is the eagle's, lightens forth
> Controlling majesty:

Here are four primacies applied to Richard: Fire, Sun, Eye, Eagle. He is also described later in the play as Rose and Lion.

Richard himself fully accepts his character as Sun-King with the lion heart. 'Lions,' he says to Mowbray, 'make leopards tame.' When Gaunt provokes him, it is an attack on the blood in the royal countenance.

> 'Dar'st with thy frozen admonition
> Make pale our cheek, chasing the royal blood
> With fury from his native residence.'

When Aumerle complains that Bolingbroke grows strong while the king does nothing, Richard replies:

> 'Discomfortable cousin! know'st thou not
> That, when the searching eye of heaven is hid
> Behind the globe and lights the lower world,
> Then thieves and robbers range abroad unseen
> In murders and in outrage bloody here.
> But when from under this terrestrial ball
> He fires the proud tops of the eastern pines
> And darts his light through every guilty hole,
> Then murders, treasons and detested sins,
> The cloak of night being pluck'd from off their backs,
> Stand bare and naked, trembling at themselves?
> So when this thief, this traitor, Bolingbroke . . .
> Shall see us rising in our throne, the east,
> His treasons will sit blushing in his face
> Not able to endure the sight of day.'*

It follows naturally that God, who enjoys the primacy of heaven, will stand by his regent on earth, and fight on Richard's side.

* Act III, Scene 2.

25

'For every man that Bolingbroke hath press'd
To lift shrewd steel against our golden crown,
God for his Richard hath, in heavenly pay,
A glorious angel . . .'

It is only when we recognise how deeply Richard feels this harmony between things heavenly and things terrestrial that we realise also the pathos in the scene at Pomfret, where the fallen king, desperately clinging to some idea of correspondence, is trying to work out a similitude between his prison and the world.

'I have been studying how I may compare
This prison where I live unto the world:
And for because the world is populous,
And here is not a creature but myself,
I cannot do it. Yet I'll hammer it out.'*

There is a foretaste in the same passage of the famous 'degree' speech in *Troilus*:

'Music do I hear?
Ha, ha! keep time: how sour sweet music is
When time is broke and no proportion kept!
So is it in the music of men's lives.' . . .

It is the same cry as: 'Untune that string'. . .

The development in the two parts of *Henry IV* (1597 and 1598) and *Henry V* (1599) is from the mediaeval monarchy of primacies to the modern monarchy of affability and efficiency, and from a divided to a united England. The two go together. In *Henry IV* faction and racial differences still divide the country. The hard-headed north countryman, Hotspur, despises the Welsh mysticism of Glendower; they are only united in their hatred of Bolingbroke.

* Act V, Scene 5.

26

Glend.	'at my nativity
	The front of heaven was full of fiery shapes,
	Of burning cressets; and at my birth
	The frame and huge foundation of the earth
	Shaked like a coward.
Hot.	Why, so it would have done at the same season, if your mother's cat had but kittened, though yourself had never been born.
Glend.	I say the earth did shake when I was born.
Hot.	And I say the earth was not of my mind
	If you suppose as fearing you it shook!
Glend.	The heavens were all on fire, the earth did tremble.
Hot.	O, then the earth shook to see the heavens on fire,
	And not in fear of your nativity. . . .
Glend.	I can call spirits from the vasty deep.
Hot.	Why, so can I, or so can any man;
	But will they come when you do call for them?

In *Henry V* the racial differences still survive. There is little love lost between Fluellen and Captain Jamy and Williams. But differ as they may they are all united in one determination —to fight for their common king. It is Prince Hal who has wrought this change, and Prince Hal who is the binding link in the three plays.

Richard may claim in a moment of poetic dejection that he is no better than his subjects ('I live with bread like you') but he despises Bolingbroke for his courtship of the common people ('Off goes his bonnet to an oyster wench').

Prince Hal not only courts them, he lives with them and likes them. Yet, as Professor Dover Wilson has pointed out, he is never entirely of them. For these historical plays also are still living in an old tradition, and they have much about them of the mediaeval morality play. The virtuous prince had to go through the toils of temptation; but he had to triumph, and the audience had to know that he would triumph, in order that they might safely enjoy the sowing of his wild oats. Hence comes the necessity of the speech at the beginning of his career, which sounds so priggish to modern ears:

> 'I know you all and will a while uphold
> The unyoked humour of your idleness:
> Yet herein will I imitate the sun,
> Who doth permit the base contagious clouds
> To smother up his beauty from the world,
> That, when he please again to be himself,
> Being wanted, he may be more wonder'd at.'

Knowing that the ship will come safe to harbour, we can settle down to enjoy the perils of the voyage.

This doubtful affability in the Prince is turned to virtue in the King. It enables him to do, what Richard could never have done, to move before Agincourt among the common soldiers, talk their language and gather their opinions. What does he discuss with them? Nothing other than the question of individual responsibility. The king is not to be responsible for his subject's souls, or even for their deaths, if they die in battle. Every man is to be responsible for himself. This mood is echoed by the soldier Williams, who tells the King (in effect) that if he comes talking to the rank and file in disguise he must take the consequences. Here is no abasement before a Sun-King. The popular monarchy is born, and we think of Charles II eating the common sailors' dinner (as observed by Mr. Pepys) on the ship that brought him home from his travels.

As in all the earlier plays there is little development of character in the Histories. Like the plays of the Greek stage they chiefly deal in *types*—the lover, the friend, the schemer, the nit-wit, the drunkard, the ideal lady, the Sun-King, the dissolute Prince, the valiant young king. Indeed in an age when producers have endeavoured to ginger Shakespeare up by presenting him in modern clothes and contemporary forms, when Hamlet can shoot Polonius behind the arras with a sub-machine gun and Artemidorus type his warning to Caesar on a portable in the streets of Rome, it is surprising that no one has put the clock back instead of forward and given us the early plays, as the Greeks would have given them, in masks. Henry V would have to change his mask before coming out from his coronation, but for the rest a single mask would do pretty well.

Yet there is one character whom a mask ought to fit and yet somehow would not; who, we feel, would keep on putting it to one side with a grin and saying, This is not me really! He is the first pure individual whom Shakespeare creates, of whom we feel we never quite know what he will say or do, but it will always be a spontaneous creation, Sir John Falstaff. The other characters are Apollinian and archetypal. Falstaff is Dionysian and individual. He first unites in himself the qualities, which the Greek drama had to keep apart because only the achieved ego can unite them, comedy and tragedy. He shows a development, even if it is a development of degradation. He tempts, but he also educates, the Prince—the rôle of the devil in the Morality and in life. But after his claim to have killed Hotspur he becomes too gross and degraded to be seen in company with the Prince, who has chosen Fortitude and Justice. But at his rejection, when his inflated hopes are punctured like a child's balloon, we want to cry rather than laugh. The description of his death is all the more tragic for its comedy.

Hostess

Nay, sure, he's not in Hell: he's in Arthur's bosom, if ever man went to Arthur's bosom. A' made a finer end and went away, an it had been any christom child; a' parted even just between twelve and one, even at the turning of the tide: for after I saw him fumble with the sheets, and play with flowers, and smile upon his fingers' ends, I knew there was but one way; for his nose was as sharp as a pen, and a' babbled of green fields. 'How now, Sir John!' quoth I: 'what, man, be o' good cheer.'

So a' cried out, 'God, God, God!' three or four times. Now I, to comfort him, bid him a' should not think of God; I hoped there was no need to trouble himself with any such thoughts yet. So a' bade me lay more clothes on his feet: I put my hands into the bed and felt them, and they were as cold as any stone; then I felt to his knees, and they were cold as any stone, and so upward and upward, and all was as cold as any stone.

The picture of the cold creeping up from the extremities may even remind us of the death of Socrates—and he also was called a Silenus. It is a fitting end for one of Shakespeare's greatest characters—indeed the first of his unique characters. But how wise Shakespeare was to kill him. 'It was always yet the trick of our English nation, if they have a good thing, to make it too common.'*

There are two fully authentic comedies (not adaptations) belonging to this first period, *Love's Labour's Lost* and *A Midsummer Night's Dream*, and of these the former is generally acknowledged to be among the earliest, if not the earliest, of the plays entirely written by Shakespeare. Dr. Rowse has claimed that it was written for the circle which paid court to Shakespeare's patron, the Earl of Southampton, and even that Berowne (in love with a dark lady) is a self-portrait of the dramatist himself. Professor Edgar Wind has shown that it contains many allusions to the kind of neo-platonic thought which had come to England from Italy, and which could well have been cultivated in such a circle. There are references to such things as the blindness of love indicating the seeing of the mind, and 'ripeness' depending on the union of opposites, which are of the essence of Renaissance Platonism. Even the cannon to which Armado refers: 'Sweet smoke of rhetoric! He reputes me a cannon': is an emblem of *festina lente*, the union of slow deliberation and quick action.

* Henry IV. Part 2, Act I, Sc. 2.

It is the play of a young writer rejoicing in the exuberance of language. Yet even here Shakespeare shows his instinctive good judgement. In Elizabeth's reign the form of English was far from fixed. There was the danger that scholars might ossify the language with too many Latin words, and constructions not adapted to an uninflected speech. There was the counter danger, represented by Euphuism, of an ornate language, full of flowery allusions and balanced antitheses, and watered with showers of alliteration. Shakespeare parodies the one in the schoolmaster Holofernes. 'Most barbarous intimation! Yet a kind of insinuation, as it were, in via, in way of explication: facere, as it were, replication, or rather ostentare, to show his inclination . . . to insert again my haud credo for a deer.' The other is burlesqued in the 'fantastical Spaniard', Don Armado, with his attendant page, who has caught the trick also from his master. 'Warble, child, make passionate my sense of hearing.' 'Adieu valour, rust rapier, be still, drum; for your manager is in love; yea, he loveth.'

Shakespeare steers his course between Scylla and Charybdis. In doing so may he not be said to have created the language we still try to speak?

A Midsummer Night's Dream—Fairies, Lovers, an Athenian Duke with his Amazonian Queen, and a classical play acted with great seriousness by British workmen in a wood a good deal nearer Stratford-on-Avon than Athens—what a magnificent charade for a wedding night! The lovers' tiffs—both of mortals and fairies—only set off the abounding good humour of the play. The high spirits are perhaps a little more *solid* than in *Love's Labour's Lost*, but there is only one really serious passage, telling us of the scope of the poet's eye between heaven and earth, and the power of the poet's pen to give shape to the unknown.

Theseus
> The poet's eye, in a fine frenzy rolling,
> Doth glance from heaven to earth, from earth to heaven,
> And as imagination bodies forth
> The forms of things unknown, the poet's pen
> Turns them to shapes, and gives to airy nothing
> A local habitation and a name.

The passage is interesting as containing perhaps the earliest use of the word imagination as meaning a creative faculty and not merely a picture of the mind, though in the whole speech the Duke hovers between the two meanings. But the play is entirely innocent of metaphysical powers, and it is only when we reach Prospero that we find airy nothing being given a local habitation and a name. And what a long way it is from the artless wood near Athens to the wisdom-filled island of *The Tempest*!

We shall not hear the seas breaking on that magical island until we have explored the whole microcosm which is Man. Very soon even the Comedies begin to bear witness to the fact that all is not well with this 'beauty of the world'. A jarring note tells us that he is no longer at home with himself or with nature. We hear it in the bitter underplot of *Much Ado about Nothing* (1598). It comes a year later in the Forest of Arden, where troubles attend both Courtier and Clown, and where wrestling is no sport for ladies. Then it sounds in the cruel treatment of Malvolio in *Twelfth Night* (probably 1600) and the uneasy presence of sot and drunkard in a fine lady's household.

It is at this point that we have three plays in which a new character first appears, the character who is withdrawn from the action, and stands aside and comments on it, in fact the Spectator. Sarcastic but kindly in the melancholy Jaques, contemptuous in Casca, vindictive in Thersites, he appears in variations on the same theme in plays as different as *As You Like It* (1599), *Julius Caesar* in the same, and *Troilus and Cressida* in the following year. They are all studies leading to the supreme picture of the Spectator in *Hamlet*.

Hamlet

Hamlet (1601) is the play of Shakespeare which the world will never leave alone. 'It seems,' wrote Lord Shaftesbury in 1710, 'most to have affected English hearts, and has perhaps been oftenest acted.' It is so universal that everyone finds in it what he wants. Critics are in complete disagreement as to the central character. The Romantic School (Goethe, Coleridge, etc.) find that Hamlet's conduct can only be justified by a state of mind bordering on insanity. Others assert that outer circumstances fully justify Hamlet's actions, or failure to act. Mr. T. S. Eliot considers that Hamlet's conduct lacks sufficient motive, and that the play is therefore an artistic failure. Professor C. S. Lewis regards the play as a profound poem, and thinks that critics who judge it on character, motives, etc., are barking up very minor trees.* Mr. Ernest Jones develops, with much ingenuity, the Freudian interpretation that Hamlet is in love with his mother, and it is his sense of a common guilt which delays his vengeance on his uncle. Perhaps the variety of judgements is the best proof of the greatness of the play.

We are, however, looking at the play not in isolation, but in the perspective of the developing picture of man in the sequence of all the plays. From this point of view the Play is a vivid picture of the Spectator Consciousness. Professor Lewis has

* *Hamlet, the Prince or the Poem.* Annual Shakespeare Lecture, British Academy, 1942.
  I am greatly indebted to this Paper, which also touches on *The Merchant of Venice*.

remarked* that as in no other play of Shakespeare 'the characters are all watching one another, listening, contriving, full of
anxiety'. Others have had the feeling that they are seeing the
whole play through Hamlet's eyes and mind, that he is always
there, looking, even when he is not visible on the stage. If
Professor Dover Wilson is right, the picture of the Spectator is
enhanced at one point of the play to the third power. For the
stage direction for the 'Play within the Play' is that it shall be
acted first in dumb show and then with the words. Professor
Wilson regards this as fully justified. For the audience want
first of all to see the play, while the King has not yet arrived;
then, with a full knowledge of the action, they can concentrate
their eyes on Hamlet and the King, while their ears hear the
words of the play. Thus the audience will look at Hamlet,
while Hamlet looks at the King, and the King looks at the Play
—three degrees of spectatorship.

We are today so accustomed to the 'spectator' attitude to life,
the looking at a world completely outside us to which we feel
we do not essentially belong, that it is difficult for us to realise
that in *Hamlet* Shakespeare is mediating a new type of consciousness into human experience. It is a consciousness which is
localised in the brain and nerves, one which is so natural to us
today that we only think it slightly ridiculous when we read
that former ages ascribed consciousness to the heart, or the
liver or the reins. The Egyptians indeed regarded the brain as
of so little importance that they threw it away when they
mummified the body and preserved the life organs. It was
Descartes who finally limited consciousness to the brain alone.
But in doing this he was perhaps not so much discovering an
absolute truth as describing a contemporary event, the final
stage of the passing from the participating consciousness
(related more nearly to the heart), to the spectator conscious-

* *Op. cit.*

ness, which—at any rate in its first manifestations—is bound to the brain. Among simpler peoples the conviction that the heart is the seat of consciousness still survives. When C. G. Jung was doing field research with the Pueblo Indians, they informed him that in their opinion the Americans were mad. The reason given was hardly one a modern mind would expect. The Americans, said the Indians, say that a man thinks with his head, 'while we know that he thinks with his heart'.

The intellectual consciousness of the head brings with it an exactness of thinking about the external world (especially mathematical thinking) and an accuracy of perception of that world unknown to other modes of consciousness. But it does so by separating the observer from the object. The feeling perception of the heart unites observer and observed. The Indian astronomer can say: 'Sometimes I put out my hand and touch a star.' His western counterpart can only calculate its distance or analyse its light.

Hamlet is in fact an imaginative, pictorial and dramatic representation of the transition from one form of consciousness to another. Hamlet himself is represented to us as originally a young man fully participating in life, an extrovert, a boon companion, accomplished in all the arts and graces of life. Then comes the shock, however we may interpret it, which makes him a spectator of the scene around him. This new attitude alters his whole picture of the world and man. The mediaeval world, born out of 'correspondences', turns for him into something like the modern world. For it is not only a personal disillusionment, but a world disillusionment which Hamlet is expressing in that great prose speech to Rosencrantz and Guildenstern* :

> 'I have of late—but wherefore I know not—lost all my mirth, forgone all custom of exercises; and indeed it goes so heavily

* Act II, Scene 2.

35

with my disposition that this goodly frame, the earth, seems to me a sterile promontory; this most excellent canopy, the air, look you, this brave o'erhanging firmament, this majestical roof fretted with golden fire, why, it appears no other thing to me than a foul and pestilent congregation of vapours. What a piece of work is a man! how noble in reason! how infinite in faculty! in form and moving how express and admirable! in action how like an angel! in apprehension how like a god! the beauty of the world! the paragon of animals. And yet, to me, what is this quintessence of dust?'

Here we have the old and the new picture of the world and of man. The 'goodly frame' has become a 'sterile promontory'— are we not told today that life on the earth is a minute interlude between aeons of lifeless existence? 'The majestical roof fretted with golden fire'* has become a 'congregation of vapours'—and the picture of Descartes' Vortices or the Kant-Laplace nebulae rises to the mind. Man 'in action how like an angel, in apprehension how like a god' has become 'the quintessence of dust'—that is the highest manifestation of the physical, which, for the most part, he now believes himself alone to be, not a kind of angel or god, a tenth hierarchy, for there are no angels or gods, not the paragon, the 'pattern of supreme excellence'† to the animals, but a pedigree animal himself. Look here upon this picture, Hamlet is saying, and on this.

One highly significant feature of the whole play is that it is full of images of dying and death.‡ If *The Merchant of Venice* is a meditation on metals, *Hamlet* is even more a meditation on death. The Ghost returns from the world of the dead and tells

* cf. Lorenzo's speech in *The Merchant of Venice:*
  'Look how the floor of heaven
  Is thick inlaid with patines of bright gold.'
† Definition in Shorter English Dictionary.
‡ See Owen Barfield, *Romanticism comes of age.* Also C. S. Lewis, *Op. cit.*

of the state of purgatory. 'Will you walk out of the air?', asks Polonius. 'Into my grave,' Hamlet replies. The Player King enacts the death of Priam. Hamlet soliloquises on suicide and the sleep of death. Murder is twice enacted in the Play within the Play. Hamlet will not kill the king at his prayers—the moment of death must be weighed. A convocation of politic worms are at Polonius. A king may go a progress through the guts of a beggar. Ophelia is drowned (or drowns herself) and may only receive maimed rites. The grave diggers exchange riddles on gallows and tombs. A tanner will last you nine year in the grave, but we have many pocky corses nowadays that will scarce hold the laying in. And all this cavalcade of death leads to the crowning picture of Hamlet standing in the grave with a skull in his hand.

Is this preoccupation not only with death but with the state of being dead merely fortuitous or has it something to do with Hamlet's spectator consciousness? I believe the two are intimately linked, because after long investigation and experience I accept to the full that relation of the powers of thought, feeling and will to three systems of the human organism described and developed in many of his works by Rudolf Steiner.* In this threefold account of man Steiner follows the accepted relation of thinking—that is modern conceptual thinking—to the brain and nervous system, though he is unique in holding, not that the brain creates thinking but that thinking creates the brain. To this brain and nerve system, however, Steiner adds another two, which are commonly regarded as performing only organic functions, but which he insists are also the physical basis for psychical powers. They are the rhythmic system, centred in heart and lungs, but radiating throughout the body, which system is the vehicle of *feeling*;

* See especially the volume of lectures to teachers published under the title *Study of Man*.

and the limb and metabolic system—all that concerns independent or irregular movement—which is the vehicle of what Steiner calls *will*. He distinguishes sharply the depth of relation between the physical and psychic elements in each of the three systems, an exact and localised relation between thinking and the brain, a looser connection between feeling and the heart, and loosest of all between the limb system and the will. This is why we are at our most conscious in thinking and at our least conscious in willing, with feeling occupying a middle position. Steiner also introduces a time dimension, in which the forces of thinking enter more from the past, those of willing from the future, while in pure feeling we have the most intense experience of the present. There is also a further polarity between the system of brain and nerves and that of limbs and metabolism, in that in the latter the force of life predominates and in the former a perpetual death process. For the brain and nerve system in man consists of substance which is perpetually dying. It is precisely because here no life forces are at work that consciousness in thinking can become so clear and acute, but is also so withdrawn from actual experience of the living world. This withdrawn consciousness is the spectator consciousness of which we have so clear a picture in *Hamlet*. The play is a 'meditation on death' for no other reason than that it is a picture of the consciousness that uses the forces of death in man. The reason why Hamlet delays action is neither state-craft nor madness. He is living too intensely in that experience which is the polar opposite of the will. It is the modern consciousness. *Hamlet* is prophetic of the modern outlook on the world, and shows us the predicament in which we all stand.

> 'The time is out of joint: O cursed spite
> That ever I was born to set it right.'

It is the cry of the angry young man who looks on the world

38

around him (for which he feels himself not responsible) and likes it not. But the Spectator consciousness detaches all men not only from nature but also from the forces in human nature. It is of the essence of the modern outlook for man to feel himself in the grip of what he believes to be impersonal forces, over which he has no control and to which he is not intrinsically related. He has yet to learn that the world-drama is played out on the stage of his own thought, feeling and will.

Lear

Lear comes five years after *Hamlet* in 1606, when Shakespeare was forty-two, with *Othello* lying midway between the two. King Lear is the opposite pole to Prince Hamlet. He lives in the instinctive powers of the will. He echoes Caesar's 'The cause is in my will—I will it so'. He acts out of impulse without thought or judgement. He has no real reason for dividing his kingdom, for distrusting Cordelia, for dismissing Kent. 'He hath ever but slenderly known himself' we are told of him. The Play shows us the painful path he has to tread before he reaches knowledge and self-knowledge.

Charles Lamb held that *Lear* could not and should not be put on the stage—it goes beyond what actors can represent or auditors dare behold. I confess that whenever I see it acted there is one scene during which I have to shut my eyes—the scene of the putting out of Gloucester's eyes. The Greeks knew better than to allow Oedipus to pierce his eyeballs on the open stage. It was at one performance of *Lear*, when, with eyes firmly closed, I was mentally praying that the agonising scene might soon be over, that the play suddenly appeared to me in a new light, as a study in seeing and blindness, physical and spiritual. Lear cannot see which is his true daughter. Gloucester, his counterpart, cannot see which is his true son. Cordelia has all the will forces of her father ('what I will intend, I'll do't before I speak') but she has raised them to the level of intuition. She sees what Lear cannot see, and takes leave of her sisters with the words

> 'with wash'd eyes
> Cordelia leaves you: I know you what you are'.

The theme of the play is the washing of the eyes of Lear.

There is almost as much about eyes and sight in *Lear* as there is about death and dying in *Hamlet*.

Kent
> See better, Lear, and let me still remain
> The true blank of thine eye.

Clown
> Why does a man's nose stand in the middle of his face?
> Why, to keep one's eyes of either side's nose, that what a man cannot smell out, he may spy into.

Gloucester (after the blinding scene)
> I have no way, and therefore want no eyes;
> I stumbled when I saw.

Lear himself
> A man may see how this world goes with no eyes.
> My eyes are not of the best.
> Does Lear walk thus? speak thus? Where are his eyes?
> Get thee glass eyes and like a scurvy politician seem
> To see the things thou dost not.
> If thou wilt weep my fortunes, take my eyes.

Gloucester has to lose his eyes in order to win spiritual sight. The passionate Lear has to come to the brink of madness in order to find sanity and himself. But he is worn out in the process. Lear achieves consciousness, as Hamlet achieves action, only at the moment of death.

Keats experienced the play of *Lear* as a kind of initiation by fire. He had to steel himself with a sonnet before entering again into the agonies of that tormented spirit.

> 'once again the fierce dispute
> Betwixt Hell torment and impassion'd clay
> Must I *burn* through . . . . . .
> But when I am consumed with the *Fire*,
> Give me new Phoenix-wings to fly at my desire.'

This is how he approached another reading of *Lear*. The impassioned will is a storm-gatherer and the elements respond to it. The whole play of *Lear* is overshadowed by the coming of the most gigantic storm ever imagined by man. The very words crack and hiss and growl as they rive the air.

> 'Blow, winds and crack your cheeks! rage! blow!
> You cataracts and hurricanoes, spout
> Till you have drench'd our steeples, drown'd the cocks!'

Even at the beginning of the play, we feel the stormy will of man calling the tempest into being out of the future. How different is the elemental background to *Hamlet*. Thinking demands stillness. The brain is the cold still pole of man's organism. So *Hamlet* begins at midnight, the hour of initiation, on the high platform under the frosty stars. The voices of the guard ring clear as crystal in the freezing air.

> 'For this relief much thanks: 'tis bitter cold,
> And I am sick at heart.'
> 'Have you had quiet guard?'
> 'Not a mouse stirring.'

Something of this cold stillness blows from the past through the entire play. It could be played in black and white without the warmth of colour. It is a play of nerves. We live in a fever of excitement but it is an intellectual fever, not the fever of passion and will. The storm conjured from the future by the impassioned will—the cold stillness playing from the past into the conscious mind—Shakespeare is true to the time dimensions of these contrasting poles of the human soul.

41

Othello

Between these two great imaginations of thinking and will lies the study of the man of heart, *Othello*. In our day we still commonly follow the Victorian tradition in thinking of the man of heart as the lover alone. But Shakespeare's age knew that the man of heart was also the man of courage, the soldier with the *coeur de lion*. It was not enough to have all virtues and graces, as Sir Philip Sidney had, unless you could prove yourself on the field of war. Othello, therefore, is essentially the man of heart, being both soldier and lover. He wins Desdemona by tales

'Of hair-breadth 'scapes i' the imminent deadly breach.'

There is no sound of the elements blowing through the play, but the noise of war and 'battle's magnificently stern array'. It is at a midnight council of war that Othello first proclaims his love. He wins the special permission of the Senate to carry Desdemona with him to Cyprus, the theatre of the war. The action of the play is against a background of active service.

As in *Hamlet* and *Lear* we are dealing in *Othello* with the virtue, and anti-virtue, of one of the great powers of the soul. Thinking should achieve certainty: when it fails of its aim, it results in agonising doubt. Willing should lead to noble action: when it goes astray, it turns inward and leads to raging madness. The love of the heart should beget knowledge of the loved one: warped into its opposite, it leads to blind misunderstanding. It is in this third reversal that we find the greatest and ultimate corruption of man. There is something admirable even in the agonies of doubt, something awe-inspiring in the violence of madness. But the corruption of love into jealousy and perversion has nothing we can commend: it is not human but satanic. That is why *Othello* is the one play of Shakespeare in which there appears a devil, Iago, who pursues evil for its own sake, who has said to himself, like Milton's Satan, 'Evil, be thou my good'. At the end of the play, when jealousy has done its work of destruction, and Othello is confronted with Iago, he looks, half-expectantly, for the cloven hoof.

> 'I look down towards his feet; but that's a fable.
> If that thou be'st a devil, I cannot kill thee.'

And a few speeches later:

> 'Will you, I pray, demand that demi-devil
> Why he hath thus ensnar'd my soul and body?'

Othello is the only play of Shakespeare in which a woman is murdered on the stage, and that not by stabbing but by the direct attack on the rhythm of life itself, where human feeling is sustained and fostered.

Caesar and Macbeth

Between *Hamlet* and *Lear* Shakespeare is at the height of his powers but also at the depth of his disillusionment. Even the comedies of this period, *All's Well that Ends Well* and *Measure for Measure*, portray the grim and the revolting. The latter has the strongest echo of Hamlet's preoccupation with the world of the dead.

Claudio
> Ay, but to die, and go we know not where;
> To lie in cold obstruction and to rot;
> This sensible warm motion to become
> A kneaded clod; and the delighted spirit
> To bathe in fiery floods, or to reside
> In thrilling region of thick-ribbed ice;
> To be imprison'd in the viewless winds,
> And blown with restless violence round about
> The pendent world;'

43

The imagination of death now goes no further than the elements. There is nothing here of the angel or the god in man. Nothing of the 'great world' to which man used to belong. Indeed in these middle plays Shakespeare represents man as reaching to the supernatural, believing, or half-believing, or not believing, in its shows and portents, but never to a true spiritual world. In this respect two plays make a remarkable contrast, the one at the beginning, the other at the end of this period. In *Julius Caesar* (1599) the whole of the supernatural world seems concentrated on the sole task of warning Caesar *not* to go to the Capitol. Graves open, men on fire walk the streets, a slave's hand burns like twenty torches, a lion roars and a lioness whelps in the Capitol, blood falls from warriors fighting in the clouds, Calpurnia thrice dreams that Caesar is murdered, the augurers find no heart in the sacrificial bird, a soothsayer arrives to give a last warning—there is no end to the portents and prodigies aimed at deterring Caesar from leaving his house. Caesar refuses to listen to any of them, and because he refuses meets his death. In *Macbeth* (1606) we have the opposite picture. Macbeth listens to the supernatural voices, and because he listens he wakens in himself the evil forces which lead him to his doom. Caesar is a man before his time playing the part of the self-contained and self-responsible ego-being in an age when instinctive forces still properly related man to nature. Macbeth is a man behind his time. He listens to the supernatural in a later age when its voices were decadent and could not truly speak to the new self-sufficient consciousness. Having once listened to the witches Macbeth cannot sustain this consciousness and falls back into the world of visions and dreams. No other play of Shakespeare is so much concerned with dreams as this. Macbeth and Lady Macbeth lose the power to sleep—the true entry into the spiritual world—and live, waking and sleeping, in the visionary dream world of a decadent clairvoyance. But the picture consciousness no longer reaches a true spiritual world as it did when in the infancy of man it produced the treasures of mythology. It has truck only with ghosts and apparitions and black magic. The Banquet scene can even appear as a ghastly travesty of the Last Supper. Macbeth gives the materialist's grace, 'Now good digestion wait on appetite', before he sits at the middle of the table. But the cup which he raises is not the cup of salvation. It brings only the ghost of Banquo, the vision of death. Perhaps even the crude symbolism by which the witches cheat Macbeth may have something of a hidden meaning. The kind of picture-clairvoyance to which he reverts belongs to the stream of the blood, of the man who is born of woman. The power that overcomes this hereditary principle is the ego power through which a man belongs not to his sisters and his brothers but to the spiritual world itself. Macduff, who is not 'born of woman' must triumph over the principle of blood.

DECLINE OF MAN

It seems that in the wonderful succession of plays from *Caesar* to *Macbeth** Shakespeare is finding and demonstrating that man cannot find his way when he is guided only by the powers of his earthly humanity. At any rate there is a progression by which the tragedy of the plays arises less and less from outward circumstances and more and more from inner defects. Caesar suffers through his greatness, not through his imperfections. Hamlet has no flaw in his character. He is caught in the net of outward circumstance. Othello is sorely attacked from without, but he has in him the latent quality of suspicion, a tinder which is all too easily kindled. And has he

* Written between the ages of 35 and 42.

not relied on an Egyptian charm—the handkerchief—to bind together what only the spirit should join?

In Lear we have a man who brings his tragedy on himself through his blindness and wilfulness. Macbeth's ruin also springs entirely from the inner flaw of his character. He falls immediately for the suggestion of the witches. Lady Macbeth may be needed to spur him on to the deed, but thought and wish are there already in abundance.

Lear and Macbeth are reputed to belong to the same year (1606). In the following year Shakespeare returns to Rome with Antony and Coriolanus, both representing noble but flawed characters whose imperfections bring ruin on themselves. Timon, said to be of the same year, is as savage a picture of human folly and depravity as has ever been painted. Timon is a corollary to Socrates. (It is Alcibiades whom Shakespeare represents as deciphering the inscription on his tomb.) He also considers that the sickness of life mends with the coming of death. But death comes not as healer, but as destroyer. Extinction is the greatest hope of man. On Timon's tomb is to be no pious Siste viator.

> 'Here lie I, Timon: who, alive, all living men did hate:
> Pass by, and curse thy fill; but pass, and stay not here
> thy gait.'

It is the full and ultimate rejection of life and man.

Shakespeare could go no further than Timon in presenting a picture of disillusionment and despair. The Spectator consciousness of the intellect has reached its end. It looks at all things and finds that they are empty and evil. There is only one thing it can now do. It can take 'the longest stride of soul man ever took'.* It can transform itself into imaginative consciousness.

* Christopher Fry: A Sleep of Prisoners.

This is in reality the step which Coleridge endeavoured to bring about at the beginning of last century. The picture of the universe acknowledged in the middle ages, indeed in all history up to modern times, had been one which man could enter into, as philosopher, as poet, as artist, with all his heart and mind and soul. The new mathematical physics had made another picture which was hardly a picture at all, but an abstraction, a mechanical universe in which impersonal forces operated in empty space. By the end of the eighteenth century men were just beginning to realise what they had done in creating this mechanical universe into which man could only properly insert himself if he also became a machine. Blake poured derisive scorn on the rational intellectual world of Locke, Newton and Johnson. To Pope's 'God said let Newton be and all was light' he retorted:

'God us keep
From single vision and Newton's sleep.'

In order to create a world into which they could fully enter, the leading spirits of the age summoned into being a new faculty, that of the conscious creation of pictures, and they called it Imagination. Blake himself regarded Imagination as the divine principle.

'O Human Imagination, O Divine Body I have crucified.'*

Wordsworth, Shelley, Keats, Goethe—all in their different ways are poets of the new Imagination, all believing that poetic vision is needed to apprehend reality. But in England the philosopher of the new belief was Coleridge, the man who was always thinking about thinking. Briefly, Coleridge, like Goethe, was deeply opposed to the belief, current both in his age and ours, that mind is a purely subjective entity born to contemplate

* Jerusalem.

47

an objective world outside it. Such an idea is a natural result of the 'Spectator' soul which Coleridge saw exemplified in the Newtonian system. 'Mind,' he wrote, 'in his (Newton's) system is always passive—a lazy looker-on at an external world. If the mind be not passive, if it be indeed made in God's image, and that, too, in the sublimest sense, the Image of the Creator, there is ground for suspicion that any system built on the passiveness of the mind must be false as a system.'*

Coleridge is of course here describing the mind as passive in the sense that it makes its connection with the world it contemplates passively—not that there is no activity in the mind itself however isolated from the world. It was this passivity of connection with the world which Coleridge set out to deny.

> 'O Lady, we receive but what we give,
> And in our thought alone does Nature live.'

The sword with which he girded himself to slay the dragon of passivity was the sword of Imagination.

It would take us too far to discuss the distinction Coleridge made between Primary and Secondary Imagination. He calls *Primary* Imagination 'the living power and prime agent of all human perception, and a repetition in the finite mind of the eternal act of creation in the infinite 'I am'. † To understand the difference which he found between Imagination and Intellect we have to introduce the idea of *Polarity* on which he built so much of his thought. The entire world is built on the fundamental polarity of *sameness* and *difference*. 'The essential duality of Nature arises out of its productive unity.' A productive unity must on the one hand strive to produce another being like itself, but in the same moment and act it must strive to overcome the detachment which it has created. This

* Letter to Poole, No. XLVI in the Nonesuch Coleridge.
† Biographia Literaria: Cap XIII.

relation of sameness and difference is not only the relation of man to God, it is also the relation of man to the world in every moment of perception. But while intellect grasps only the *difference*, Imagination apprehends both *sameness* and *difference*. To think in abstractions with the intellect may (and does) give us power over nature but cannot give us insight into her. It is when we begin to think in *pictures* that we take the first step to overcoming the dichotomy of man and the world by introducing the element of sameness into what hitherto has been mere difference. For the picture is the manifestation in the finite mind of 'the eternal act of creation in the infinite "I am".' That is why Coleridge warned his generation of the danger of thinking without pictures. It is Imagination which gives meaning. Without it words become counters or symbols, as in the case of the mathematical view of the universe. All you can say is that in certain circumstances the symbols work. But they have no meaning. They cannot produce a universe into which man can insert himself as man.

But should we say that there were no mental pictures before the age of the Romantics? On the contrary, in the early history of man there was, I believe, little else. But then the pictures sprang from an instinctive consciousness, a clairvoyant consciousness if you will, by which men apprehended the world not in clearly defined sense pictures but in dream images that revealed the quality and essence of the thing, or the divine being informing it, rather than what we would call today the thing itself. But these dream images were given, just as the sense pictures are given to us today every time we open our eyes. The last memory of these dream images was in the 'correspondences' which we have seen were still an active, though a dying experience in the time of Shakespeare. The eighteenth century delighted in comparing one thing with another ('I think that is a pretty good image, Sir' said Boswell

49

when he had likened himself and Johnson to a small and big bottle). But such comparisons are quite external, and altogether different from the pictures of Imagination which have inner unifying, moulding power—Coleridge had the temerity to call it 'esemplastic'—which enriches, enlivens and even takes part in the creation of the thing pictured.

It is to such creative, enlivening and enriching pictures that we are brought in the last three fully authentic plays of Shakespeare, written in 1610 and 1611, *Cymbeline, The Winter's Tale* and *The Tempest*. But before we reach them we have one of the strangest of all the Plays, the only one that belongs to the years 1608 and 1609, *Pericles, Prince of Tyre*. It is not so much a play as a series of pictures. The moral Gower, from whom Shakespeare took the story, appears as Prologue, and several times, not content with mere verbal pictures, calls for a dumb show to illustrate events occurring between the actual scenes of the play. There can hardly be said to be a plot, or what plot there is merely serves to bring about a series of romantic episodes as improbable, as inconsequent and as vivid as the events of a dream. But there are the realistic scenes in a bawdy house—as degraded as anything Shakespeare ever drew—to remind us that we are still in contact with the world of fallen humanity. Some of the episodes remind us of earlier plays but not a few anticipate the plays yet to come. The opening is a kind of travesty of the caskets of Belmont. All wooers of the daughter of Antiochus have to solve a riddle—or lose their heads. Pericles guesses the answer to the riddle, that Antiochus has committed incest with his daughter. Such is the initial plot or *primum mobile* of the play, with which even *Cymbeline* can hardly vie in unpleasantness. In consequence, Pericles has to leave his city, appointing Helicanus to rule it for him, as the Duke appoints Angelo in *Measure for Measure*. Pericles relieves a famine in Tarsus, but the agents of Antiochus still pursue him, and he leaves Tarsus 'until our stars that frown, lend us a smile'—the language of Hermione and Prospero. He is shipwrecked, and some of the description of the storm reminds us of *The Tempest*. Indeed the sea is always sounding in the background of both plays alike. After the shipwreck he wins the daughter of the local king—it is love at first sight as with Ferdinand and Miranda, and the king feigns the same anger with the lovers as does Prospero in *The Tempest*. Pericles next hears that Antiochus is dead and he can return to Tyre, but again he encounters a storm, in which his wife dies in childbirth. Her body is caulked up in a chest and thrown overboard, but is washed up at Ephesus, where a noble magician—a kind of prototype for Prospero—brings her back to life, and places her in the Temple of Diana. Pericles leaves his newborn child —Marina—to be brought up by his friend Cleon of Tarsus, who has a daughter of the same age, and the two become another Celia and Rosalind. But Cleon and his wife are jealous for their daughter (as happens also in *As You Like It*) and he and his wife conspire to murder Marina (his wife is the stronger character and upbraids her husband for hesitation somewhat like Lady Macbeth). Marina escapes murder through being seized by pirates, and is sold to a bawdy house in Mitylene where, however, she maintains her chastity, and indeed becomes the Wonder of Mitylene for her accomplishments. Pericles goes to visit his daughter in Tarsus but is shown her tomb by the wicked Cleon and his wife. In the extremity of his grief he goes dumb, but on the return journey his ship puts in at Mitylene where the Governor opines that the Wonder of Mitylene may cure him. Not only do father and daughter discover each other, but Diana appears to Pericles in a vision (as Jupiter appears in *Cymbeline*) and tells Pericles to visit her temple at Ephesus, where his recognition of his wife in the Priestess of Diana is reminiscent of the Statue scene in *The Winter's Tale*.

51

I have ventured on this synopsis because the play is little read and was generally considered unactable until a recent performance at Stratford proved (it is said) the contrary. I think it is plain to anyone who allows this bewildering series of pictures to pass before his mind that we are here living in quite a different state of consciousness from that which produced *Lear*, or *Antony*, or *Timon*. It is the inauguration of a sort of 'thinking in pictures' which makes the last plays of Shakespeare comparable to Fairy Tales, but only if we grant that the pictures of Fairy Tales conceal and reveal much of the essential depths and riches of life.

THE LAST THREE PLAYS

It was the view of Victorian critics that after the *sturm und drang* of *Hamlet*, *Lear* and *Othello* Shakespeare amused his serene old age with the charming Fairy Tales of *Cymbeline*, *The Winter's Tale* and *The Tempest*. They seem to have overlooked the fact that there is no more beastly plot than that of *Cymbeline* and no more degraded character than Cloten, that both Leontes and Polixenes in *The Winter's Tale* behave with tyrannical cruelty, that it is hard to imagine a more depraved collection of men than are gathered together on the ship which was wrecked on the magic island of *The Tempest*—murderers, cut-throats, traitors, drunkards and lechers. Indeed, apart from the Prince, there is only one decent man among them, and he is a bore. Nor does the language reveal a placid spirit. It has been well noted that in the earlier plays Shakespeare's language is often over exuberant, too many words chasing too little meaning; that in the middle plays meaning and language fit like the acorn in its cup; while in the last plays the meaning is often in such haste to be born that it twists and distorts the language, leaving phrases incompleted and making hay with grammar and syntax. Like lightning, it rives the oak through which it has to find its way to the ground. It is not serenity or charm which constitutes the Fairy Tale element in these last plays, it is that more than in any plays of Shakespeare they evoke and speak through the magic of pictures. We see this even in the Songs. The Songs in *As You Like It* have meaning in the ordinary sense. The Songs of *The Tempest* have no meaning. They enchant us into visions.

But there is also another element common to these last three plays which differentiates them from the epoch of the great tragedies. It is that Shakespeare is transcending the picture of Death. Death is an essential part of Life and cannot be ultimately ignored. In the great Tragedies, the powers out of which men direct their affairs are inadequate to solve the tangle into which human relations have fallen. The only solution—a great and beneficial solution—is death. Indeed we should be grateful to death that it is continually solving human problems. Tragedy accepts and uses Death. Comedy ignores it by the convention of the 'happy ending'. Is there a third way of treating Death? I believe there is, and that in different degrees and depths the last three plays exemplify a way of transcending death. It is by the representation in the whole picture of the play of a power superior to death, a consciousness able to redeem the ordinary death-consciousness in man, whether coming from a world beyond man, or working as a force of resurrection in man himself.

The first essay in such a representation appears in the first of the last three plays, *Cymbeline*. Here the drug which takes away the senses of Imogen leads not, as in the case of Juliet, to death, but to the resurrection of life and the restoration to husband and father. But this is not the main thing. By the end of the fourth act human affairs are in such a desperate state that it would seem the only solution is the Tragic solution of Death. But in the fifth act Shakespeare reverts to that ancient device of the Greek stage, the *Deus ex Machina*. Posthumus, in prison, sees in a visionary dream the ghosts of his dead parents and brothers conjure Jupiter to descend from the heavens and set human affairs to rights. Jupiter descends on an eagle, places a tablet on the breast of Posthumus, and reascends into the skies. The oracle written on the tablet—a series of appalling plays on words—restores Imogen to Posthumus and both to Cymbeline.

The revival of the *Deus ex Machina* is as unsatisfactory as the oracle itself is crude. If we may judge by the doggerel in which most of the act is written, Shakespeare himself was somewhat contemptuous of his own solution. Indeed it was difficult to imagine a more unsatisfactory fifth act until Mr. Bernard Shaw obliged by writing an alternative one. But we can at least say that the Play presents a picture of communication between man and a divine world, however crudely represented, and this communication is brought about by the spirits of the dead. (We should remember that no representation of the Christian Trinity or the traditional hierarchies was permitted on the Elizabethan Stage; also that the word 'ghost' had not yet lost touch with its original simple meaning of the soul of a dead person.) We can indeed experience—especially after witnessing the coming to life of Imogen—a kind of resurrection in human affairs in the play, although the machinery is external and does not penetrate and inform the play itself. But it does present us with the picture of a divine world able and willing, at the intercession of man, to enter into and guide human affairs on the earth.

The Winter's Tale

In some respects *Cymbeline* can be compared to *Lear*. Both

54

plays represent British Kings who are blind to the merits of a daughter. Of all Shakespeare's heroines Imogen stands nearest to Cordelia. But in a far deeper sense *The Winter's Tale* may be compared to *Othello*. The theme of jealousy is the same, that perversion of love through which the eye distorts and the heart misrepresents. But *The Winter's Tale* reaches at the end of the second act the catastrophe which comes at the end of *Othello*. Before the third act Leontes has murdered an innocent wife through jealousy. Of course Hermione is not really murdered, but Leontes is none the less guilty for that. Indeed he is worse than Othello, for he gives orders for his friend Polixenes to be poisoned, and for his new-born baby first to be burnt, but afterwards to be exposed. His violence causes the actual death of his elder child, as he believes it has caused—and indeed as it should have caused—that of his queen.

Into this woeful scene of death there gradually enters the force of resurrection. It begins, where *Cymbeline* ended, with an oracle. But this time the oracle brings conviction both by the way it is presented and by the magnificent language in which Cleomenes and Dion, the two messengers to Delphi, describe the scene in the Temple.

Dion

                    I shall report,
For most it caught me, the celestial habits,—
Methinks I so should term them,—and the reverence
Of the grave wearers. O, the sacrifice!
How ceremonious, solemn, and unearthly
It was i' the offering!

Cleomenes

                    But of all, the burst
And the ear-deafening voice o' the oracle,
Kin to Jove's thunder, so surpris'd my sense
That I was nothing.

After that, we cannot but listen with conviction to the oracular voice.

But this is only a beginning. We land on the sea-coast of Bohemia and there we find the 'murdered' child of Hermione come to life as a shepherdess in the most exquisite pastoral Shakespeare, or any poet, ever wrote. Perdita comes before us at the sheep-shearing feast holding the flowers of middle summer, but calling for the flowers of spring.

> 'O Proserpina!
> For the flowers now that, frighted, thou let'st fall
> From Dis's wagon! daffodils
> That come before the swallow dares, and take
> The winds of March with beauty; violets dim,
> But sweeter than the lids of Juno's eyes
> Or Cytherea's breath; pale primroses,
> That die unmarried, ere they can behold
> Bright Phoebus in his strength . . . . .'

As she says these words, Perdita herself, with her arms full of flowers, appears as the Spring Goddess of Resurrection, the picture of the yearly overcoming of the cold forces of death, the happy ending to every Winter's Tale.

We then take ship (from the sea-coasts of Bohemia) and in Sicily we experience a human resurrection scene, the restoration of Hermione to life. Well acted this scene can be as moving and as magical as anything in Shakespeare. We feel it in terms of the words in which Paulina speaks to the reborn Hermione.

> 'Come;
> I'll fill your grave up: stir; nay, come away;
> Bequeath to death your numbness, for from him
> Dear life redeems you.'

Like the sacrifice at Delphi, the scene of resurrection is

'ceremonious, solemn and unearthly'.

A spiritual force is revealing itself not from without but in the structure and picture of the play itself. The tragic ending of death is transcended by the picture of resurrection.

The Tempest

The Tempest is the play which, more than any others, has been described and discussed in recent years as a 'Mystery' Play. The opening situation is precisely parallel to *Hamlet*. A reigning prince has been murdered by his brother who has usurped his kingdom. The fact that Prospero was not actually killed makes no difference to the guilt of the brother, Antonio. For he had commanded that Prospero and Miranda be taken out to sea, placed in the 'rotten carcass of a butt' without sail or tackle, or food or water, and left to a certain death. It was through the faithful Gonzalo alone that they survived. But what vengeance shall be taken on the murderer?

As in *Hamlet*, therefore, we are facing a question of Justice. Indeed there is a sense in which all the great stories of the world are about justice, and, generally speaking, virtue is rewarded and evil brings its own retribution. This is almost invariably so in Fairy Tales where the virtuous prince wins the beautiful princess and the wicked witch is rolled down the hill in a barrel full of spikes. On a larger scale, the virtuous Pandus in the Mahabharrata finally defeat the crafty and treacherous Kurus. Rama recovers his bride in the Ramayana, and Odysseus in the Odyssey. In the Iliad, the death of Patroclus is avenged, even if we may not like the manner of the vengeance. Even when the hero is slain, as Roland is slain, death brings greater glory than life. Shakespeare stands in this old tradition, not in the sense that the innocent in his plays never suffer, but in that evil is never made to triumph, and is practically always

57

punished. It is therefore important to notice how he deals with the problem of evil in this last of his plays.

I have mentioned that the basic plot of *The Tempest* is the same as in *Hamlet*. But there is another drama long preceding *Hamlet* dealing with a very similar situation, the story of Agamemnon, Clytemnestra and Orestes. In this story, as has already been mentioned in connection with *Romeo and Juliet*, there is no question of the duty of Orestes to avenge his father by killing the murderer, in this case his mother. Hamlet is in doubt even as to his uncle; he has the direct command of the ghost, his father, *not* to kill his mother. With her he goes about the matter in another way, her punishment is to be brought to know what she has done. 'Have you eyes?' reiterates Hamlet, and his mother replies:

> 'Thou turn'st mine eyes into my very soul'.

It is a foretaste of the vengeance taken, or punishment inflicted, by Prospero on his brother. Antonio, and his fellow conspirators, Alonso and Sebastian, are brought to the island so that they may become conscious of what they have done. Alonso finds the record of his deed written in the elements.

> 'O, it is monstrous, monstrous!
> Methought the billows spoke, and told me of it;
> The winds did sing it to me; and the thunder,
> That deep and dreadful organ pipe, pronounced
> The name of Prosper.'

Ariel has told them that nothing will save them from 'lingering perdition' but 'heart-sorrow and a clear life ensuing'. And Gonzalo comments

> 'their great guilt,
> Like poison given to work a great time after,
> Now gins to bite the spirits'.

It is a picture of what will ultimately become the true object and nature of punishment—to make the criminal fully realise what he has done. It is not a light punishment. Shakespeare represents it as driving Alonso to the verge of madness.

We may indeed regard *The Tempest* as a 'meditation on justice' at this ordinary human level. But it is the virtue of a myth—and *The Tempest* is of this calibre—that it flourishes in all climates and seasons, and flowers on the mountain and in the valley alike. On one occasion *The Tempest* spoke to me in an unforgettable manner of a greater representation of justice than the one we have been considering. It was when I saw it performed against the background of a lake. Water has many possibilities. Your goddesses can arrive gliding smoothly on a punt. And on this occasion at the end of the Play, Prospero conducted his guests not only to his study which Caliban had suitably trimmed (we hope) for the occasion, but afterwards to the good and gallant ship which the boatswain had reported tight and yare as when they first put to sea. As, to soft music, the royal vessel moved out to sea, Caliban came shaking his fists on the shore, and, by what Shakespeare would have called a quaint device, Ariel ran out over the waters kissing hands in farewell. Then, as the ship began to round an island in the lake, Prospero leaned over the side and drowned his book 'deeper than did ever plummet sound'. The actors had gone back to Naples and Milan and the busy earth. We were left on the magic island. Where is that magic island?, I asked myself; and in asking I suddenly experienced the play as a picture of the greatest of all spheres of justice, where it is not limited to the few years of a single life on earth but works through threads of destiny that bind centuries and milleniums together in the story of the individual as well as of mankind. It is a picture of justice familiar to the ancient and modern east, and far from unknown in the west, which holds that the unsatisfied desires and unfulfilled, or wrongly fulfilled, possibilities of one life draw the immortal spirit again into another. It is the picture which Plato drew in the Myth of Er at the end of his great treatise on justice, *The Republic*. For something still needed to be said, after the just City had been built, of justice for the individual, and Plato tells us of Er, the son of Armenius, who was left for dead on the field of battle and accompanied the souls of those who had died on their journey: but, restored to life, he was able to tell of those ascending on their planetary journey and of those descending who went to choose their lot in a new life: and, that justice might be done, each one chose a life which compensated for his former one. It is the picture which led the Jews to send to John the Baptist to ask what prophet he was, and Christ to ask his disciples: Who do men say that I am? It is the picture to which among others of the western world the modern scientific seer, Rudolf Steiner, has returned again and again, but always with the new Christian emphasis on the need for the individual to share through Christ in the task of redemption of mankind and of the earth.

So I experienced the island of *The Tempest*, as a spiritual place where those who had passed through death learnt as in a kind of purgatory to know themselves, and to seek a new destiny on earth with those whom they had wronged. Certain of the speeches then rang with a new force in my mind.

Ariel's speech to the murderers:

> 'You are three men of sin, whom Destiny—
> That hath to instrument this lower world
> And what is in 't—the never-surfeited sea
> Hath caused to belch up you; . . . .
>   You fools! I and my fellows
> Are ministers of Fate . . . . .'

Gonzalo
                              O, rejoice
Beyond a common joy! and set it down
With gold on lasting pillars. In one voyage
Did Claribel her husband find at Tunis,
And Ferdinand, her brother, found a wife
Where he himself was lost; Prospero his dukedom
In a poor isle; *and all of us ourselves,*
When no man was his own.'

I do not of course mean that Shakespeare set out in dramatic
form a treatise on justice as it operates from life to life in what
the East calls Karma. He was a great artist writing a great play
about men and women in the form of a romantic myth. But the
play is also a meditation on justice, and, because it is such, that
deepest aspect of justice, which even Plato chose only to
represent in a myth, shines through the story to an age which is
again beginning to interest itself in Myth and Mystery and
which is everywhere seeking for paths of spiritual experience.
Hamlet was the great play for the age of the Spectator Consciousness. As this age recedes and men enter a new and
conscious union with the spiritual forces in and behind nature,
they will perhaps turn more and more to the last plays and
especially to *The Tempest*. For there they will find the picture of
communication with the divine, of the overcoming of the forces
of death in human consciousness, of man realising himself as a
spirit in a world of spiritual beings.

Much mystical thought underlay the works of art of the
Renaissance which has been overlooked in the age of reason,
as is slowly being rediscovered today. How many of us have
looked at Botticelli's *Primavera* and imagined that Hermes on
the left of the picture is picking apples? But now Professor
Wind* with his delicate scholarship shows us that the uplifted

* *Op. cit.*

hand of Hermes is really parting the clouds which separate the human from the divine world. As Hermes is the psychopomp, may we not say that he is preparing to lead the soul again into a spiritual world? Renaissance Platonism, as has been said, appears in specific allusions in the earlier plays. In the latest it has entered into their very flesh and blood.

Shakespeare was also a truly Renaissance figure in that he loved Courts and Great Houses, where the Renaissance man felt that life could be really lived, as the Greeks felt it of the City State and Samuel Johnson of Charing Cross. Only three of his Plays are enacted mainly or entirely against a Nature background, *A Midsummer Night's Dream*, *As You Like It*, and *The Tempest*. In the first—one of the earliest of the plays, the wood near Athens is full of elemental beings, the last denizens of the world of spirits accessible to man. It is they who pull the strings while the mortals are the puppets who dance to their tune. *As You Like It*, which ushers in the second period of the plays, is also mainly enacted in a wood, the Forest of Arden. But there are no fairies in the wood. Instead Nature is always resounding with the human art of music. There is no play so filled with songs. Jaques is the modern intellectual who finds his great solace in music, and he is for ever calling for a song. At his first entry, Amiens sings 'Under the greenwood tree'. 'More, more, I prithee, more' is Jaques' comment, and throughout the play we have more. 'Blow, blow, thou winter wind', 'It was a lover and his lass', 'What shall he have that kill'd the deer'—there is nothing of this human music in the *Dream*. And in *The Tempest* it is not the mortals who sing and make music, but Ariel, or the cloud of spirits which is Ariel. They are ever creating the element in which they live, the ethereal music which Caliban too acknowledges:

> 'Be not afeared: the isle is full of noises,
> Sounds and sweet airs, that give delight, and hurt not'.

Earthly music is the solace for Jaques because it bears within it the memory of the heavenly music of the spheres. Adam and Eve had no need of music in the Paradisal garden because they walked with spiritual beings. It was when men lost their dreamlike perception of the spirit that Art was given them as a memory and a consolation.* If they find their true destiny they will walk again with spiritual beings, but consciously and as sharers in their powers. This is the picture of Prospero, the last picture of man which Shakespeare gave us. Indeed he could go no further, for in painting it he had plumbed the ultimate depth of the secret of man. Fittingly, therefore, he buried his staff 'certain fathoms in the earth', and drowned his book 'deeper than did ever plummet sound'.

The lower elements—earth and water—could receive no more.

* See Rudolf Steiner: *Metamorphoses of the Soul.*